~ Raging ~ Psychedelic ~

Random Thoughts ~ Sights ~ Favorite Songs ~ Insane Jams ~ Doodles ~ Lawn ~ Friends ~

Bass Bombs ~ LOVE ~ Musings ~ Shakedown ~ Memories ~

Sketches ~ Riding the Rail ~ Dancing ~ Twirling ~ Teases ~ Merch ~ Posters ~ P

MW01201783

5

On The Road To The Show

Date

I started out in

Travelled by   for   hours and   miles

Travelled with

and arrived in

I stayed at

Road Trip Playlist

Memories From The Road

Lodging Notes

BAND

Venue	Date
Location	Day of the week
Opening Act(s)	Show # of a
I hung out with	night run
	Seat Location

SET 1

SET 2

Encore / SET 3

Rating ☆ ☆ ☆ ☆ ☆

Tour ~ Lights ~ Fellowship ~ Raging ~ Psychedelic ~ Source ~ Pins ~ Posters ~ Merch ~ Teases ~ Twirling ~ Dancing ~ Riding the Rail ~ Sketches ~ Memories ~ Shakedown ~ Musings ~ LOVE ~ Bass Bombs ~ Friends ~ Lawn ~ Doodles ~ Insane Jams ~ Favorite Songs ~ Sights ~ Random Thoughts ~

Random Thoughts ~ Sights ~ Favorite Songs ~ Insane Jams ~ Doodles ~ Lawn ~ Friends ~

Bass Bombs ~ LOVE ~ Musings ~ Shakedown ~ Memories ~

Sketches ~ Riding the Rail ~ Dancing ~ Twirling ~ Teases ~ Merch ~ Posters ~ Pins ~ Sound ~

Tour ~ Lights ~ Fellowship ~ Raging ~ Psychedelic ~

On The Road To The Show

Date

I started out in

Travelled by   for   hours and   miles

Travelled with

and arrived in

I stayed at

Road Trip Playlist

Memories From The Road

Lodging Notes

BAND

	Date
Venue	Day of the week
Location	Show # of a
Opening Act(s)	night run
I hung out with	Seat Location

SET 1

SET 2

Encore / SET 3

Rating ☆ ☆ ☆ ☆ ☆

~ Tour ~ Lights ~ Fellowship ~ Raging ~ Psychedelic ?

Random Thoughts ~ Sights ~ Favorite Songs ~ Insane Jams ~ Doodles ~ Lawn ~ Friends ~

Bass Bombs ~ LOVE ~ Musings ~ Shakedown ~ Memories

Sketches ~ Riding the Rail ~ Dancing ~ Twirling ~ Teases ~ Merch ~ Posters ~ Pins ~ Sound

~ Tour ~ Lights ~ Fellowship ~ Raging ~ Psychedelic ~

Random Thoughts ~ Sights ~ Favorite Songs ~ Insane Jams ~ Doodles ~ Lawn ~ Friends ~

Sound ~ Pins ~ Posters ~ Merch ~ Teases ~ Twirling ~ Dancing ~ Riding the Rail ~ Sketches ~

Bass Bombs ~ LOVE ~ Musings ~ Shakedown ~ Memories ~

On The Road To The Show

Date

I started out in

Travelled by   for   hours and   miles

Travelled with

and arrived in

I stayed at

Road Trip Playlist

Memories From The Road

Lodging Notes

BAND

	Date
Venue	Day of the week
Location	Show # of a
Opening Act(s)	night run
I hung out with	Seat Location

SET 1

SET 2

Encore / SET 3

Rating ☆ ☆ ☆ ☆ ☆

~ Tour ~ Lights ~ Fellowship ~ Raging ~ Psychedelic ?

Random Thoughts ~ Sights ~ Favorite Songs ~ Insane Jams ~ Doodles ~ Lawn ~ Friends ~

~ Tour ~ Sounds ~ Pins ~ Posters ~ Merch ~ Teases ~ Twirling ~ Dancing ~ Riding the Rail ~ Sketches ~

Bass Bombs ~ LOVE ~ Musings ~ Shakedown ~ Memories

Random Thoughts ~ Sights ~ Favorite Songs ~ Insane Jams ~ Doodles ~ Lawn ~ Friends ~

~ Tour ~ Lights ~ Fellowship ~ Raging ~ Psychedelic ~

Sound ~ Pins ~ Posters ~ Merch ~ Teases ~ Twirling ~ Dancing ~ Riding the Rail ~ Sketches ~

Bass Bombs ~ LOVE ~ Musings ~ Shakedown ~ Memories

On The Road To The Show

Date

I started out in

Travelled by   for   hours and   miles

Travelled with

and arrived in

I stayed at

Road Trip Playlist

Memories From The Road

Lodging Notes

BAND

	Date
Venue	Day of the week
Location	Show # of a
Opening Act(s)	night run
I hung out with	Seat Location

SET 1

SET 2

Encore / SET 3

Rating ☆ ☆ ☆ ☆ ☆

~ Tour ~ Lights ~ Fellowship ~ Raging ~ Psychedelic ~

Random Thoughts ~ Sights ~ Favorite Songs ~ Insane Jams ~ Doodles ~ Lawn ~ Friends ~

Sounds ~ Pins ~ Posters ~ Merch ~ Teases ~ Twirling ~ Dancing ~ Riding the Rail ~ Sketches ~

Bass Bombs ~ LOVE ~ Musings ~ Shakedown ~ Memories

Random Thoughts ~ Sights ~ Favorite Songs ~ Insane Jams ~ Doodles ~ Lawn ~ Friends ~

Bass Bombs ~ LOVE ~ Musings ~ Shakedown ~ Memories

Sketches ~ Riding the Rail ~ Dancing ~ Twirling ~ Teases ~ Merch ~ Posters ~ Pins ~ Sound

~ Tour ~ Lights ~ Fellowship ~ Raging ~ Psychedelic

On The Road To The Show

Date

I started out in

Travelled by   for   hours and   miles

Travelled with

and arrived in

I stayed at

Road Trip Playlist

Memories From The Road

Lodging Notes

BAND

Date

Venue

Day of
the week

Location

Show #   of a

Opening Act(s)

night run

I hung out with

Seat
Location

SET 1

SET 2

Encore / SET 3

Rating ☆ ☆ ☆ ☆ ☆

~ Tour ~ Lights ~ Fellowship ~ Raging ~ Psychedelic ?

Random Thoughts ~ Sights ~ Favorite Songs ~ Insane Jams ~ Doodles ~ Lawn ~ Friends ~

Sounds ~ Pins ~ Posters ~ Merch ~ Teases ~ Twirling ~ Dancing ~ Riding the Rail ~ Sketches ~

Bass Bombs ~ LOVE ~ Musings ~ Shakedown ~ Memories

Tour ~ Lights ~ Fellowship ~ Raging ~ Psychedelic ~

Random Thoughts ~ Sights ~ Favorite Songs ~ Insane Jams ~ Doodles ~ Lawn ~ Friends ~

Bass Bombs ~ LOVE ~ Musings ~ Shakedown ~ Memories

Sketches ~ Riding the Rail ~ Dancing ~ Twirling ~ Teases ~ Merch ~ Posters ~ Pins ~ Sound ~

On The Road To The Show

Date

I started out in			
Travelled by	for	hours and	miles
Travelled with			
and arrived in			
I stayed at			

Road Trip Playlist

Memories From The Road

Lodging Notes

BAND

Date

Venue

Day of
the week

Location

Show #   of a

Opening Act(s)

night run

I hung out with

Seat
Location

SET 1

SET 2

Encore / SET 3

Rating ☆ ☆ ☆ ☆ ☆

Random Thoughts ~ Sights ~ Favorite Songs ~ Insane Jams ~ Doodles ~ Lawn ~ Friends ~

Bass Bombs ~ LOVE ~ Musings ~ Shakedown ~ Memories

~ Sketches ~ Riding the Rail ~ Dancing ~ Twirling ~ Teases ~ Merch ~ Posters ~ Pins ~ Sound

~ Tour ~ Lights ~ Fellowship ~ Raging ~ Psychedelic ~

Random Thoughts ~ Sights ~ Favorite Songs ~ Insane Jams ~ Doodles ~ Lawn ~ Friends ~ Bass Bombs ~ LOVE ~ Musings ~ Shakedown ~ Memories ~ Sketches ~ Riding the Rail ~ Dancing ~ Twirling ~ Teases ~ Merch ~ Posters ~ Pins ~ Sounds ~ Tour ~ Lights ~ Fellowship ~ Raging ~ Psychedelic ~

On The Road To The Show   Date

I started out in

Travelled by   for   hours and   miles

Travelled with

and arrived in

I stayed at

Road Trip Playlist

Memories From The Road

Lodging Notes

BAND

	Date
Venue	Day of the week
Location	Show # of a
Opening Act(s)	night run
I hung out with	Seat Location

SET 1

SET 2

Encore / SET 3

Rating ☆ ☆ ☆ ☆ ☆

Random Thoughts ~ Sights ~ Favorite Songs ~ Insane Jams ~ Doodles ~ Lawn ~ Friends ~

~ Tour ~ Lights ~ Fellowship ~ Raging ~ Psychedelic ?

Sounds ~ Pins ~ Posters ~ Merch ~ Teases ~ Twirling ~ Dancing ~ Riding the Rail ~ Sketches ~

Bass Bombs ~ LOVE ~ Musings ~ Shakedown ~ Memories

Random Thoughts ~ Sights ~ Favorite Songs ~ Insane Jams ~ Doodles ~ Lawn ~ Friends ~

Bass Bombs ~ LOVE ~ Musings ~ Shakedown ~ Memories ~

Sketches ~ Riding the Rail ~ Dancing ~ Twirling ~ Teases ~ Merch ~ Posters ~ Pins ~ Sounds ~

Tour ~ Lights ~ Fellowship ~ Raging ~ Psychedelic ~

On The Road To The Show

Date

I started out in

Travelled by   for   hours and   miles

Travelled with

and arrived in

I stayed at

Road Trip Playlist

Memories From The Road

Lodging Notes

BAND

	Date
Venue	Day of the week
Location	Show # ___ of a
Opening Act(s)	___ night run
I hung out with	Seat Location

SET 1

SET 2

Encore / SET 3

Rating ☆ ☆ ☆ ☆ ☆

~ Tour ~ Lights ~ Fellowship ~ Raging ~ Psychedelic ?

Random Thoughts ~ Sights ~ Favorite Songs ~ Insane Jams ~ Doodles ~ Lawn ~ Friends ~

~ Sound ~ Pins ~ Posters ~ Merch ~ Teases ~ Twirling ~ Dancing ~ Riding the Rail ~ Sketches ~

Bass Bombs ~ LOVE ~ Musings ~ Shakedown ~ Memories

Random Thoughts ~ Sights ~ Favorite Songs ~ Insane Jams ~ Doodles ~ Lawn ~ Friends ~ Bass Bombs ~ LOVE ~ Musings ~ Shakedown ~ Memories ~ Sketches ~ Riding the Rail ~ Dancing ~ Twirling ~ Teases ~ Merch ~ Posters ~ Pins ~ Sounds ~ Tour ~ Lights ~ Fellowship ~ Raging ~ Psychedelic ~

On The Road To The Show

Date

I started out in

Travelled by   for   hours and   miles

Travelled with

and arrived in

I stayed at

Road Trip Playlist

Memories From The Road

Lodging Notes

BAND

	Date
Venue	Day of the week
Location	Show # of a
Opening Act(s)	night run
I hung out with	Seat Location

SET 1

SET 2

Encore / SET 3

Rating ☆ ☆ ☆ ☆ ☆

Random Thoughts ~ Sights ~ Favorite Songs ~ Insane Jams ~ Doodles ~ Lawn ~ Friends ~

Bass Bombs ~ LOVE ~ Musings ~ Shakedown ~ Memories ~ Sketches ~ Riding the Rail ~ Dancing ~ Twirling ~ Teases ~ Merch ~ Posters ~ Pins ~ Sounds ~ Tour ~ Lights ~ Fellowship ~ Raging ~ Psychedelic ~

~ Tour ~ Lights ~ Fellowship ~ Raging ~ Psychedelic ~

Random Thoughts ~ Sights ~ Favorite Songs ~ Insane Jams ~ Doodles ~ Lawn ~ Friends ~

Bass Bombs ~ LOVE ~ Musings ~ Shakedown ~ Memories

Sketches ~ Riding the Rail ~ Dancing ~ Twirling ~ Teases ~ Merch ~ Posters ~ Pins ~ Sound ~

On The Road To The Show

Date

I started out in

Travelled by _____ for _____ hours and _____ miles

Travelled with

and arrived in

I stayed at

Road Trip Playlist

Memories From The Road

Lodging Notes

BAND

Venue

Location

Opening Act(s)

I hung out with

Date

Day of
the week

Show #   of a

night run

Seat
Location

SET 1

SET 2

Encore / SET 3

Rating ☆ ☆ ☆ ☆ ☆

Random Thoughts ~ Sights ~ Favorite Songs ~ Insane Jams ~ Doodles ~ Lawn ~ Friends ~ Bass Bombs ~ LOVE ~ Musings ~ Shakedown ~ Memories ~ Sketches ~ Riding the Rail ~ Dancing ~ Twirling ~ Teases ~ Merch ~ Posters ~ Pins ~ Sounds ~ Tour ~ Lights ~ Fellowship ~ Raging ~ Psychedelic ~

44

Random Thoughts ~ Sights ~ Favorite Songs ~ Insane Jams ~ Doodles ~ Lawn ~ Friends ~

~ Tour ~ Lights ~ Fellowship ~ Raging ~ Psychedelic ~

Sounds ~ Pins ~ Posters ~ Merch ~ Teases ~ Twirling ~ Dancing ~ Riding the Rail ~ Sketches ~

Bass Bombs ~ LOVE ~ Musings ~ Shakedown ~ Memories

On The Road To The Show

Date

I started out in

Travelled by   for   hours and   miles

Travelled with

and arrived in

I stayed at

Road Trip Playlist

Memories From The Road

Lodging Notes

BAND

	Date
Venue	Day of the week
Location	Show # of a
Opening Act(s)	night run
I hung out with	Seat Location

SET 1

SET 2

Encore / SET 3

Rating ☆ ☆ ☆ ☆ ☆

~ Tour ~ Lights ~ Fellowship ~ Raging ~ Psychedelic ~

Random Thoughts ~ Sights ~ Favorite Songs ~ Insane Jams ~ Doodles ~ Lawn ~ Friends ~

Sounds ~ Pins ~ Posters ~ Merch ~ Teases ~ Twirling ~ Dancing ~ Riding the Rail ~ Sketches ~

Bass Bombs ~ LOVE ~ Musings ~ Shakedown ~ Memories

48

Random Thoughts ~ Sights ~ Favorite Songs ~ Insane Jams ~ Doodles ~ Lawn ~ Friends ~ Bass Bombs ~ LOVE ~ Musings ~ Shakedown ~ Memories ~ Sketches ~ Riding the Rail ~ Dancing ~ Twirling ~ Teases ~ Merch ~ Posters ~ Pins ~ Sounds ~ Tour ~ Lights ~ Fellowship ~ Raging ~ Psychedelic ~

On The Road To The Show

Date

I started out in

Travelled by   for   hours and   miles

Travelled with

and arrived in

I stayed at

Road Trip Playlist

Memories From The Road

Lodging Notes

BAND

Date

Venue

Day of the week

Location

Show #   of a

Opening Act(s)

night run

I hung out with

Seat Location

SET 1

SET 2

Encore / SET 3

Rating ☆ ☆ ☆ ☆ ☆

~ Tour ~ Lights ~ Fellowship ~ Raging ~ Psychedelic ~

Random Thoughts ~ Sights ~ Favorite Songs ~ Insane Jams ~ Doodles ~ Lawn ~ Friends ~

Sounds ~ Pins ~ Posters ~ Merch ~ Teases ~ Twirling ~ Dancing ~ Riding the Rail ~ Sketches ~

Bass Bombs ~ LOVE ~ Musings ~ Shakedown ~ Memories

Random Thoughts ~ Sights ~ Favorite Songs ~ Insane Jams ~ Doodles ~ Lawn ~ Friends ~

~ Tour ~ Lights ~ Fellowship ~ Raging ~ Psychedelic ~

Sketches ~ Riding the Rail ~ Dancing ~ Twirling ~ Teases ~ Merch ~ Posters ~ Pins ~ Sounds

Bass Bombs ~ LOVE ~ Musings ~ Shakedown ~ Memories

On The Road To The Show

Date

I started out in

Travelled by   for   hours and   miles

Travelled with

and arrived in

I stayed at

Road Trip Playlist

Memories From The Road

Lodging Notes

BAND

	Date
Venue	Day of the week
Location	Show # of a
Opening Act(s)	night run
I hung out with	Seat Location

SET 1

SET 2

Encore / SET 3

Rating ☆ ☆ ☆ ☆ ☆

~ Tour ~ Lights ~ Fellowship ~ Raging ~ Psychedelic ~

Random Thoughts ~ Sights ~ Favorite Songs ~ Insane Jams ~ Doodles ~ Lawn ~ Friends ~

Sound ~ Pins ~ Posters ~ Merch ~ Teases ~ Twirling ~ Dancing ~ Riding the Rail ~ Sketches ~

Bass Bombs ~ LOVE ~ Musings ~ Shakedown ~ Memories

Tour ~ Lights ~ Fellowship ~ Raging ~ Psychedelic

Random Thoughts ~ Sights ~ Favorite Songs ~ Insane Jams ~ Doodles ~ Lawn ~ Friends ~

Sounds ~ Pins ~ Posters ~ Merch ~ Teases ~ Twirling ~ Dancing ~ Riding the Rail ~ Sketches ~

Bass Bombs ~ LOVE ~ Musings ~ Shakedown ~ Memories

On The Road To The Show

Date

I started out in

Travelled by   for   hours and   miles

Travelled with

and arrived in

I stayed at

Road Trip Playlist

Memories From The Road

Lodging Notes

BAND

Venue	Date
Location	Day of the week
Opening Act(s)	Show # ___ of a ___ night run
I hung out with	Seat Location

SET 1

SET 2

Encore / SET 3

Rating ☆ ☆ ☆ ☆ ☆

Random Thoughts ~ Sights ~ Favorite Songs ~ Insane Jams ~ Doodles ~ Lawn ~ Friends ~

Bass Bombs ~ LOVE ~ Musings ~ Shakedown ~ Memories

Sketches ~ Riding the Rail ~ Dancing ~ Twirling ~ Teases ~ Merch ~ Posters ~ Pins ~ Sounds

~ Tour ~ Lights ~ Fellowship ~ Raging ~ Psychedelic

~ Tour ~ Lights ~ Fellowship ~ Raging ~ Psychedelic ~

Random Thoughts ~ Sights ~ Favorite Songs ~ Insane Jams ~ Doodles ~ Lawn ~ Friends ~

Sounds ~ Pins ~ Posters ~ Merch ~ Teases ~ Twirling ~ Dancing ~ Riding the Rail ~ Sketches ~

Bass Bombs ~ LOVE ~ Musings ~ Shakedown ~ Memories

On The Road To The Show

Date

I started out in

Travelled by   for   hours and   miles

Travelled with

and arrived in

I stayed at

Road Trip Playlist

Memories From The Road

Lodging Notes

BAND

Date

Venue

Day of
the week

Location

Show #   of a

Opening Act(s)

night run

I hung out with

Seat
Location

SET 1

SET 2

Encore / SET 3

Rating ☆ ☆ ☆ ☆ ☆

~ Tour ~ Lights ~ Fellowship ~ Raging ~ Psychedelic ~

Random Thoughts ~ Sights ~ Favorite Songs ~ Insane Jams ~ Doodles ~ Lawn ~ Friends ~

~ Sounds ~ Pins ~ Posters ~ Merch ~ Teases ~ Twirling ~ Dancing ~ Riding the Rail ~ Sketches ~

Bass Bombs ~ LOVE ~ Musings ~ Shakedown ~ Memories

Tour ~ Lights ~ Fellowship ~ Raging ~ Psychedelic

Random Thoughts ~ Sights ~ Favorite Songs ~ Insane Jams ~ Doodles ~ Lawn ~ Friends ~

Sketches ~ Riding the Rail ~ Dancing ~ Twirling ~ Teases ~ Merch ~ Posters ~ Pins ~ Sounds

Bass Bombs ~ LOVE ~ Musings ~ Shakedown ~ Memories

On The Road To The Show

Date

I started out in

Travelled by _____ for _____ hours and _____ miles

Travelled with

and arrived in

I stayed at

Road Trip Playlist

Memories From The Road

Lodging Notes

BAND

Venue	Date
Location	Day of the week
Opening Act(s)	Show # of a
I hung out with	night run
	Seat Location

SET 1

SET 2

Encore / SET 3

Rating ☆ ☆ ☆ ☆ ☆

~ Tour ~ Lights ~ Fellowship ~ Raging ~ Psychedelic ~

Random Thoughts ~ Sights ~ Favorite Songs ~ Insane Jams ~ Doodles ~ Lawn ~ Friends ~

~ Sounds ~ Pins ~ Posters ~ Merch ~ Teases ~ Twirling ~ Dancing ~ Riding the Rail ~ Sketches ~

Bass Bombs ~ LOVE ~ Musings ~ Shakedown ~ Memories ~

Random Thoughts ~ Sights ~ Favorite Songs ~ Insane Jams ~ Doodles ~ Lawn ~ Friends ~

~ Tour ~ Lights ~ Fellowship ~ Raging ~ Psychedelic ~

Sounds ~ Pins ~ Posters ~ Merch ~ Teases ~ Twirling ~ Dancing ~ Riding the Rail ~ Sketches ~

Bass Bombs ~ LOVE ~ Musings ~ Shakedown ~ Memories

On The Road To The Show

Date

I started out in

Travelled by   for   hours and   miles

Travelled with

and arrived in

I stayed at

Road Trip Playlist

Memories From The Road

Lodging Notes

BAND

Venue	Date
Location	Day of the week
Opening Act(s)	Show # of a
I hung out with	night run
	Seat Location

SET 1

SET 2

Encore / SET 3

Rating ☆ ☆ ☆ ☆ ☆

Tour ~ Lights ~ Fellowship ~ Raging ~ Psychedelic ~

~ Sound ~ Pins ~ Posters ~ Merch ~ Teases ~ Twirling ~ Dancing ~ Riding the Rail ~ Sketches ~

Random Thoughts ~ Sights ~ Favorite Songs ~ Insane Jams ~ Doodles ~ Lawn ~ Friends ~

Bass Bombs ~ LOVE ~ Musings ~ Shakedown ~ Memories

72

~ Tour ~ Lights ~ Fellowship ~ Raging ~ Psychedelic ~

Random Thoughts ~ Sights ~ Favorite Songs ~ Insane Jams ~ Doodles ~ Lawn ~ Friends ~

Sounds ~ Pins ~ Posters ~ Merch ~ Teases ~ Twirling ~ Dancing ~ Riding the Rail ~ Sketches ~

Bass Bombs ~ LOVE ~ Musings ~ Shakedown ~ Memories

On The Road To The Show

Date

I started out in

Travelled by   for   hours and   miles

Travelled with

and arrived in

I stayed at

Road Trip Playlist

Memories From The Road

Lodging Notes

BAND

Venue

Location

Opening Act(s)

I hung out with

Date

Day of
the week

Show #   of a

night run

Seat
Location

SET 1

SET 2

Encore / SET 3

Rating ☆ ☆ ☆ ☆ ☆

Random Thoughts ~ Sights ~ Favorite Songs ~ Insane Jams ~ Doodles ~ Lawn ~ Friends ~

~ Tour ~ Lights ~ Fellowship ~ Raging ~ Psychedelic '

~ Sounds ~ Pins ~ Posters ~ Merch ~ Teases ~ Twirling ~ Dancing ~ Riding the Rail ~ Sketches ~

Bass Bombs ~ LOVE ~ Musings ~ Shakedown ~ Memories '

Random Thoughts ~ Sights ~ Favorite Songs ~ Insane Jams ~ Doodles ~ Lawn ~ Friends ~

Tour ~ Lights ~ Fellowship ~ Raging ~ Psychedelic ~

Sketches ~ Riding the Rail ~ Dancing ~ Twirling ~ Teases ~ Merch ~ Posters ~ Pins ~ Sounds

Bass Bombs ~ LOVE ~ Musings ~ Shakedown ~ Memories

On The Road To The Show

Date

I started out in

Travelled by   for   hours and   miles

Travelled with

and arrived in

I stayed at

Road Trip Playlist

Memories From The Road

Lodging Notes

BAND

Venue	Date
Location	Day of the week
Opening Act(s)	Show # of a
I hung out with	night run
	Seat Location

SET 1

SET 2

Encore / SET 3

Rating ☆ ☆ ☆ ☆ ☆

Tour ~ Lights ~ Fellowship ~ Raging ~ Psychedelic ?

Random Thoughts ~ Sights ~ Favorite Songs ~ Insane Jams ~ Doodles ~ Lawn ~ Friends ~

~ Tour ~ Sounds ~ Pins ~ Posters ~ Merch ~ Teases ~ Twirling ~ Dancing ~ Riding the Rail ~ Sketches ~

Bass Bombs ~ LOVE ~ Musings ~ Shakedown ~ Memories

Random Thoughts ~ Sights ~ Favorite Songs ~ Insane Jams ~ Doodles ~ Lawn ~ Friends ~ Bass Bombs ~ LOVE ~ Musings ~ Shakedown ~ Memories ~ Sketches ~ Riding the Rail ~ Dancing ~ Twirling ~ Teases ~ Merch ~ Posters ~ Pins ~ Sounds ~ Tour ~ Lights ~ Fellowship ~ Raging ~ Psychedlic ~

On The Road To The Show   Date

I started out in

Travelled by   for   hours and   miles

Travelled with

and arrived in

I stayed at

Road Trip Playlist

Memories From The Road

Lodging Notes

BAND

Venue	Date
	Day of the week
Location	Show # of a
Opening Act(s)	night run
I hung out with	Seat Location

SET 1

SET 2

Encore / SET 3

Rating ☆ ☆ ☆ ☆ ☆

~ Tour ~ Lights ~ Fellowship ~ Raging ~ Psychedelic ~

Random Thoughts ~ Sights ~ Favorite Songs ~ Insane Jams ~ Doodles ~ Lawn ~ Friends ~

Sounds ~ Pins ~ Posters ~ Merch ~ Teases ~ Twirling ~ Dancing ~ Riding the Rail ~ Sketches ~

Bass Bombs ~ LOVE ~ Musings ~ Shakedown ~ Memories

Random Thoughts ~ Sights ~ Favorite Songs ~ Insane Jams ~ Doodles ~ Lawn ~ Friends ~ Bass Bombs ~ LOVE ~ Musings ~ Shakedown ~ Memories ~ Sketches ~ Riding the Rail ~ Dancing ~ Twirling ~ Teases ~ Merch ~ Posters ~ Pins ~ Sounds ~ Tour ~ Lights ~ Fellowship ~ Raging ~ Psychedelic ~

On The Road To The Show

Date

I started out in

Travelled by   for   hours and   miles

Travelled with

and arrived in

I stayed at

Road Trip Playlist

Memories From The Road

Lodging Notes

BAND

	Date
Venue	Day of the week
Location	Show # of a
Opening Act(s)	night run
I hung out with	Seat Location

SET 1

SET 2

Encore / SET 3

Rating ☆ ☆ ☆ ☆ ☆

Random Thoughts ~ Sights ~ Favorite Songs ~ Insane Jams ~ Doodles ~ Lawn ~ Friends ~

~ Tour ~ Lights ~ Fellowship ~ Raging ~ Psychedelic '

Bass Bombs ~ LOVE ~ Musings ~ Shakedown ~ Memories

Sketches ~ Riding the Rail ~ Dancing ~ Twirling ~ Teases ~ Merch ~ Posters ~ Pins ~ Sounds

Random Thoughts ~ Sights ~ Favorite Songs ~ Insane Jams ~ Doodles ~ Lawn ~ Friends ~

Bass Bombs ~ LOVE ~ Musings ~ Shakedown ~ Memories

Sketches ~ Riding the Rail ~ Dancing ~ Twirling ~ Teases ~ Merch ~ Posters ~ Pins ~ Sounds

~ Tour ~ Lights ~ Fellowship ~ Raging ~ Psychedelic

On The Road To The Show

Date

I started out in

Travelled by   for   hours and   miles

Travelled with

and arrived in

I stayed at

Road Trip Playlist

Memories From The Road

Lodging Notes

BAND

	Date
Venue	Day of the week
Location	Show # of a
Opening Act(s)	night run
I hung out with	Seat Location

SET 1

SET 2

Encore / SET 3

Rating ☆ ☆ ☆ ☆ ☆

~ Tour ~ Lights ~ Fellowship ~ Raging ~ Psychedelic ?

Random Thoughts ~ Sights ~ Favorite Songs ~ Insane Jams ~ Doodles ~ Lawn ~ Friends ~

Sketches ~ Riding the Rail ~ Dancing ~ Twirling ~ Teases ~ Merch ~ Posters ~ Pins ~ Sounds

Bass Bombs ~ LOVE ~ Musings ~ Shakedown ~ Memories

~ Tour ~ Lights ~ Fellowship ~ Raging ~ Psychedelic ?

Random Thoughts ~ Sights ~ Favorite Songs ~ Insane Jams ~ Doodles ~ Lawn ~ Friends ~

Bass Bombs ~ LOVE ~ Musings ~ Shakedown ~ Memories

Sketches ~ Riding the Rail ~ Dancing ~ Twirling ~ Teases ~ Merch ~ Posters ~ Pins ~ Sounds

On The Road To The Show

Date

I started out in

Travelled by   for   hours and   miles

Travelled with

and arrived in

I stayed at

Road Trip Playlist

Memories From The Road

Lodging Notes

BAND

Venue

Location

Opening Act(s)

I hung out with

Date

Day of
the week

Show #   of a

night run

Seat
Location

SET 1

SET 2

Encore / SET 3

Rating ☆ ☆ ☆ ☆ ☆

~ Tour ~ Lights ~ Fellowship ~ Raging ~ Psychedelic '

Random Thoughts ~ Sights ~ Favorite Songs ~ Insane Jams ~ Doodles ~ Lawn ~ Friends ~

Sketches ~ Riding the Rail ~ Dancing ~ Twirling ~ Teases ~ Merch ~ Posters ~ Pins ~ Sound

Bass Bombs ~ LOVE ~ Musings ~ Shakedown ~ Memories

~ Tour ~ Lights ~ Fellowship ~ Raging ~ Psychedelic ~

Random Thoughts ~ Sights ~ Favorite Songs ~ Insane Jams ~ Doodles ~ Lawn ~ Friends ~

Bass Bombs ~ LOVE ~ Musings ~ Shakedown ~ Memories

Sketches ~ Riding the Rail ~ Dancing ~ Twirling ~ Teases ~ Merch ~ Posters ~ Pins ~ Sounds

On The Road To The Show

Date

I started out in

Travelled by   for   hours and   miles

Travelled with

and arrived in

I stayed at

Road Trip Playlist

Memories From The Road

Lodging Notes

BAND

Venue	Date
	Day of the week
Location	Show # of a
Opening Act(s)	night run
I hung out with	Seat Location

SET 1

SET 2

Encore / SET 3

Rating ☆ ☆ ☆ ☆ ☆

Tour ~ Lights ~ Fellowship ~ Raging ~ Psychedelic ~

Random Thoughts ~ Sights ~ Favorite Songs ~ Insane Jams ~ Doodles ~ Lawn ~ Friends ~

Sketches ~ Riding the Rail ~ Dancing ~ Twirling ~ Teases ~ Merch ~ Posters ~ Pins ~ Sound ~

Bass Bombs ~ LOVE ~ Musings ~ Shakedown ~ Memories

Random Thoughts ~ Sights ~ Favorite Songs ~ Insane Jams ~ Doodles ~ Lawn ~ Friends ~ Bass Bombs ~ LOVE ~ Musings ~ Shakedown ~ Memories ~ Sketches ~ Riding the Rail ~ Dancing ~ Twirling ~ Teases ~ Merch ~ Posters ~ Pins ~ Sounds ~ Tour ~ Lights ~ Fellowship ~ Raging ~ Psychedelic ~

On The Road To The Show

Date

I started out in

Travelled by   for   hours and   miles

Travelled with

and arrived in

I stayed at

Road Trip Playlist

Memories From The Road

Lodging Notes

BAND

	Date
Venue	Day of the week
Location	Show # of a
Opening Act(s)	night run
I hung out with	Seat Location

SET 1

SET 2

Encore / SET 3

Rating ☆ ☆ ☆ ☆ ☆

Random Thoughts ~ Sights ~ Favorite Songs ~ Insane Jams ~ Doodles ~ Lawn ~ Friends ~

Bass Bombs ~ LOVE ~ Musings ~ Shakedown ~ Memories ~ Sketches ~ Riding the Rail ~ Dancing ~ Twirling ~ Teases ~ Merch ~ Posters ~ Pins ~ Sounds ~ Tour ~ Lights ~ Fellowship ~ Raging ~ Psychedelic ~

Random Thoughts ~ Sights ~ Favorite Songs ~ Insane Jams ~ Doodles ~ Lawn ~ Friends ~ Bass Bombs ~ LOVE ~ Musings ~ Shakedown ~ Memories ~ Sketches ~ Riding the Rail ~ Dancing ~ Twirling ~ Teases ~ Merch ~ Posters ~ Pins ~ Sounds ~ Tour ~ Lights ~ Fellowship ~ Raging ~ Psychedelic ~

On The Road To The Show

Date

I started out in

Travelled by _____ for _____ hours and _____ miles

Travelled with

and arrived in

I stayed at

Road Trip Playlist

Memories From The Road

Lodging Notes

BAND

Date

Venue

Day of
the week

Location

Show #   of a

Opening Act(s)

night run

I hung out with

Seat
Location

SET 1

SET 2

Encore / SET 3

Rating ☆ ☆ ☆ ☆ ☆

~ Tour ~ Lights ~ Fellowship ~ Raging ~ Psychedelic ?

Random Thoughts ~ Sights ~ Favorite Songs ~ Insane Jams ~ Doodles ~ Lawn ~ Friends ~

Sketches ~ Riding the Rail ~ Dancing ~ Twirling ~ Teases ~ Merch ~ Posters ~ Pins ~ Sounds ~

Bass Bombs ~ LOVE ~ Musings ~ Shakedown ~ Memories

Random Thoughts ~ Sights ~ Favorite Songs ~ Insane Jams ~ Doodles ~ Lawn ~ Friends ~ Bass Bombs ~ LOVE ~ Musings ~ Shakedown ~ Memories ~ Sketches ~ Riding the Rail ~ Dancing ~ Twirling ~ Teases ~ Merch ~ Posters ~ Pins ~ Sounds ~ Tour ~ Lights ~ Fellowship ~ Raging ~ Psychedelic ~

On The Road To The Show

Date

I started out in

Travelled by   for   hours and   miles

Travelled with

and arrived in

I stayed at

Road Trip Playlist

Memories From The Road

Lodging Notes

BAND

Venue

Location

Opening Act(s)

I hung out with

Date

Day of
the week

Show #   of a

night run

Seat
Location

SET 1

SET 2

Encore / SET 3

Rating ☆ ☆ ☆ ☆ ☆

Random Thoughts ~ Sights ~ Favorite Songs ~ Insane Jams ~ Doodles ~ Lawn ~ Friends ~

Bass Bombs ~ LOVE ~ Musings ~ Shakedown ~ Memories ~

Sketches ~ Riding the Rail ~ Dancing ~ Twirling ~ Teases ~ Merch ~ Posters ~ Pins ~ Sounds ~

~ Tour ~ Lights ~ Fellowship ~ Raging ~ Psychedelic ~

Random Thoughts ~ Sights ~ Favorite Songs ~ Insane Jams ~ Doodles ~ Lawn ~ Friends ~ Bass Bombs ~ LOVE ~ Musings ~ Shakedown ~ Memories ~ Sketches ~ Riding the Rail ~ Dancing ~ Twirling ~ Teases ~ Merch ~ Posters ~ Pins ~ Sounds ~ Tour ~ Lights ~ Fellowship ~ Raging ~ Psychedelic ~

On The Road To The Show

Date

I started out in

Travelled by   for   hours and   miles

Travelled with

and arrived in

I stayed at

Road Trip Playlist

Memories From The Road

Lodging Notes

BAND

	Date
Venue	Day of the week
Location	Show # of a
Opening Act(s)	night run
I hung out with	Seat Location

SET 1

SET 2

Encore / SET 3

Rating ☆ ☆ ☆ ☆ ☆

Tour ~ Lights ~ Fellowship ~ Raging ~ Psychedelic ~

Random Thoughts ~ Sights ~ Favorite Songs ~ Insane Jams ~ Doodles ~ Lawn ~ Friends ~

Sketches ~ Riding the Rail ~ Dancing ~ Twirling ~ Teases ~ Merch ~ Posters ~ Pins ~ Sounds ~

Bass Bombs ~ LOVE ~ Musings ~ Shakedown ~ Memories ~

~ Tour ~ Lights ~ Fellowship ~ Raging ~ Psychedelic ~

Random Thoughts ~ Sights ~ Favorite Songs ~ Insane Jams ~ Doodles ~ Lawn ~ Friends ~

Sounds ~ Pins ~ Posters ~ Merch ~ Teases ~ Twirling ~ Dancing ~ Riding the Rail ~ Sketches ~

Bass Bombs ~ LOVE ~ Musings ~ Shakedown ~ Memories

On The Road To The Show

Date

I started out in

Travelled by   for   hours and   miles

Travelled with

and arrived in

I stayed at

Road Trip Playlist

Memories From The Road

Lodging Notes

BAND

Date

Venue — Day of the week

Location — Show # — of a

Opening Act(s) — night run

I hung out with — Seat Location

SET 1

SET 2

Encore / SET 3

Rating ☆ ☆ ☆ ☆ ☆

~ Tour ~ Lights ~ Fellowship ~ Raging ~ Psychedelic ~

Random Thoughts ~ Sights ~ Favorite Songs ~ Insane Jams ~ Doodles ~ Lawn ~ Friends ~

Sounds ~ Pins ~ Posters ~ Merch ~ Teases ~ Twirling ~ Dancing ~ Riding the Rail ~ Sketches ~

Bass Bombs ~ LOVE ~ Musings ~ Shakedown ~ Memories

Random Thoughts ~ Sights ~ Favorite Songs ~ Insane Jams ~ Doodles ~ Lawn ~ Friends ~ Bass Bombs ~ LOVE ~ Musings ~ Shakedown ~ Memories ~ Sketches ~ Riding the Rail ~ Dancing ~ Twirling ~ Teases ~ Merch ~ Posters ~ Pins ~ Sounds ~ Tour ~ Lights ~ Fellowship ~ Raging ~ Psychedelic ~

On The Road To The Show

Date

I started out in

Travelled by   for   hours and   miles

Travelled with

and arrived in

I stayed at

Road Trip Playlist

Memories From The Road

Lodging Notes

BAND

	Date
Venue	Day of the week
Location	Show # of a
Opening Act(s)	night run
I hung out with	Seat Location

SET 1

SET 2

Encore / SET 3

Rating ☆ ☆ ☆ ☆ ☆

Tour ~ Lights ~ Fellowship ~ Raging ~ Psychedelic ~

Random Thoughts ~ Sights ~ Favorite Songs ~ Insane Jams ~ Doodles ~ Lawn ~ Friends ~

Sounds ~ Pins ~ Posters ~ Merch ~ Teases ~ Twirling ~ Dancing ~ Riding the Rail ~ Sketches ~

Bass Bombs ~ LOVE ~ Musings ~ Shakedown ~ Memories

Random Thoughts ~ Sights ~ Favorite Songs ~ Insane Jams ~ Doodles ~ Lawn ~ Friends ~ Bass Bombs ~ LOVE ~ Musings ~ Shakedown ~ Memories ~ Sketches ~ Riding the Rail ~ Dancing ~ Twirling ~ Teases ~ Merch ~ Posters ~ Pins ~ Sounds ~ Tour ~ Lights ~ Fellowship ~ Raging ~ Psychedelic ~

On The Road To The Show

Date

I started out in

Travelled by   for   hours and   miles

Travelled with

and arrived in

I stayed at

Road Trip Playlist

Memories From The Road

Lodging Notes

BAND

	Date
Venue	Day of the week
Location	Show # of a
Opening Act(s)	night run
I hung out with	Seat Location

SET 1

SET 2

Encore / SET 3

Rating ☆ ☆ ☆ ☆ ☆

Random Thoughts ~ Sights ~ Favorite Songs ~ Insane Jams ~ Doodles ~ Lawn ~ Friends ~

Bass Bombs ~ LOVE ~ Musings ~ Shakedown ~ Memories ~ Sketches ~ Riding the Rail ~ Dancing ~ Twirling ~ Teases ~ Merch ~ Posters ~ Pins ~ Sounds ~ Tour ~ Lights ~ Fellowship ~ Raging ~ Psychedelic ~

Tour ~ Lights ~ Fellowship ~ Raging ~ Psychedelic ~

Random Thoughts ~ Sights ~ Favorite Songs ~ Insane Jams ~ Doodles ~ Lawn ~ Friends ~

Sounds ~ Pins ~ Posters ~ Merch ~ Teases ~ Twirling ~ Dancing ~ Riding the Rail ~ Sketches ~

Bass Bombs ~ LOVE ~ Musings ~ Shakedown ~ Memories

On The Road To The Show

Date

I started out in

Travelled by   for   hours and   miles

Travelled with

and arrived in

I stayed at

Road Trip Playlist

Memories From The Road

Lodging Notes

BAND

Venue

Location

Opening Act(s)

I hung out with

Date

Day of
the week

Show #   of a

night run

Seat
Location

SET 1

SET 2

Encore / SET 3

Rating ☆ ☆ ☆ ☆ ☆

Random Thoughts ~ Sights ~ Favorite Songs ~ Insane Jams ~ Doodles ~ Lawn ~ Friends ~

Bass Bombs ~ LOVE ~ Musings ~ Shakedown ~ Memories ~

Sketches ~ Riding the Rail ~ Dancing ~ Twirling ~ Teases ~ Merch ~ Posters ~ Pins ~ Sounds ~

Tour ~ Lights ~ Fellowship ~ Raging ~ Psychedelic ~

~ Tour ~ Lights ~ Fellowship ~ Raging ~ Psychedelic ~

Random Thoughts ~ Sights ~ Favorite Songs ~ Insane Jams ~ Doodles ~ Lawn ~ Friends ~

Sounds ~ Pins ~ Posters ~ Merch ~ Teases ~ Twirling ~ Dancing ~ Riding the Rail ~ Sketches ~

Bass Bombs ~ LOVE ~ Musings ~ Shakedown ~ Memories

On The Road To The Show

Date

I started out in

Travelled by   for   hours and   miles

Travelled with

and arrived in

I stayed at

Road Trip Playlist

Memories From The Road

Lodging Notes

BAND

	Date
Venue	Day of the week
Location	Show # of a
Opening Act(s)	night run
I hung out with	Seat Location

SET 1

SET 2

Encore / SET 3

Rating ☆ ☆ ☆ ☆ ☆

Tour ~ Lights ~ Fellowship ~ Raging ~ Psychedelic ~

Source ~ Pins ~ Posters ~ Merch ~ Teases ~ Twirling ~ Dancing ~ Riding the Rail ~ Sketches ~

Random Thoughts ~ Sights ~ Favorite Songs ~ Insane Jams ~ Doodles ~ Lawn ~ Friends ~

Bass Bombs ~ LOVE ~ Musings ~ Shakedown ~ Memories

Random Thoughts ~ Sights ~ Favorite Songs ~ Insane Jams ~ Doodles ~ Lawn ~ Friends ~

Bass Bombs ~ LOVE ~ Musings ~ Shakedown ~ Memories ~ Sketches ~ Riding the Rail ~ Dancing ~ Twirling ~ Teases ~ Merch ~ Posters ~ Pins ~ Sounds

~ Tour ~ Lights ~ Fellowship ~ Raging ~ Psychedelic ~